I0471322

Manifesting Soft Power Management

(Synergized with 'Principles of Manifesting Thoughts')

Ashish Mehta

Copyright © 2013 Ashish Mehta

Ashish Mehta

ISBN-13: 978-1484156483

"Thinking"

"If you think you are beaten, you are,

If you think you dare not, you don't.

If you like to win, but you think you can't,

It is almost certain you won't.

If you think you'll lose, you're lost,

For out in the world we find,

Success begins with a fellow's will.

It's all in the state of mind.

If you think you are outclassed, you are,

You've got to think high to rise,

You've got to be sure of yourself before

You can ever win a prize.

Life's battles don't always go

To the stronger or faster man.

But soon or late the man who wins,

Is the man who thinks he can."

~ Walter D. Wintle (late 19th and early 20th century)

CONTENTS

Chapter 1

Self Assessment of your Managerial Skills

Most individuals, who are in the field of managing, have in most cases planned, worked and studied to be in this field or in some stray cases, have suddenly one fine day, found themselves in the midst of the responsibilities.

So, how did you land up in this really huge field of managing? Do you really enjoy your responsibilities or do you despise them? Do you have an inherent way of coming up with creative solutions when you suddenly face a wall of discontent or do you curl up in your corner?

The following few paragraphs are basically self-assessing in nature. It is suggested, before you carry on reading this book, on a separate piece of paper, genuinely answer these questions about yourself. You don't need to show or share this with anyone, but they would help you in understanding your own mind, your own personality much better.

So here we go:-

- In your own opinion, how powerful are you as a Manager / Leader?
- What according to you are your strengths & weaknesses?
- How do you visualize yourself as a Leader and what are the successes you yearn for?
- How do you rate yourself in Leadership qualities and Emotional Intelligence (EI) (On a scale of 1 to 10, please rate yourself as 1 for Poor & 10 for Excellent)
- Are you a team man?
- Do you lead by example?

- Are you Trustworthy in others eyes?

- Do you show Empathy towards others?

- What is the level of Self-accountability?

- How important is Appreciative Intelligence for you?

- How generous are you towards your subordinates?

- Are you a good Motivator?

- Are you satisfied with your demeanor?

- Did you have a mentor? How fondly do you remember him or her?

- How communicative are you?

- Do you trust others with a given job?

- How do you view prosperity?

- Are you humble or arrogant in your approach?

- How dignified is your behavior?

- What is your take on moral standards?

- Are you a critical person by nature?

- Are you a hard or soft task master?

If you feel you need to better yourself, which aspect or aspects in your opinion would you need to work upon? The above answers, based on your individual experiences and how you went through them, would by and large give you an idea of your strengths and of your weaknesses. This self-assessment is the biggest gift you can give yourself. And believe me, no Management-Guru would be able to help you more than you, yourself.

This book is about imbibing attributes of Soft Power in one's personality, which has been observed to help, guide and mould even managers with mediocre abilities into successful leaders. With your self-assessments now on paper with you, use specific soft power attributes to strengthen your weaknesses and further strengthen your positives too.

Chapter 2

The success of a manager

As a manager or a person at a senior level, your success depends on two virtues - (A) Doing a good job professionally and (B) Guiding and molding the human resource at your disposal towards Organizational good. The first virtue is something that you would have learnt and developed as your professional skill. We take it as pre-supposed that you know your job best. We will take up here honing of the second virtue here - the virtue of handling and optimally utilizing the human resource at your disposal.

The disposition of every individual is different. The biggest challenge faced by every Manager or Team-Leader or Head of Department, is to optimally make use of and better the resources at hand and extract the best output. Apart from having sound knowledge of his or her subject the success of the manager depends on the second virtue mentioned above. In this book, we will not only discuss these human and managerial virtues per se, we will learn how to effectively manifest these into our behavior, our professional and personal lives.

A most important human virtue is to be 'Sthitpragya'. This is a word in the hindi language and one which is found extensively in the spiritual epic "Shrimad Bhagwat Gita". It denotes being 'still' and being 'aware', apart from larger ramifications.

As humans we are subject to a lot of situations and resulting emotions of fear, anger, vindictiveness, jealousy and many more such. Every negative emotion has the tendency and the power to 'dislodge' us mentally. Being 'still' and being 'aware' helps you to observe situations from a neutral point of view. Once an individual is lodged in this mental state, he or she is able to survey all with an eagle eye, without letting emotions interfere. Hence the 'macro', 'balanced' or as is also known as a '30000 feet view approach' is possible. But this view is one which develops with time and experience. Within this one virtue are encompassed a large number of attributes, skills and mini-virtues. We shall be bringing forth the importance of manifestation of these various virtues. That is the Soft Power one would develop in executing the managerial skills.

Chapter 3

The Beauty & Efficacy of Soft Power

Soft Power is 'attractional' power. It is the power of cajoling others into following and working on the path shown by you. It is partly motivational. It is partly inspirational. It is partly out of love. It is soul-stirring. It is mentally rousing. It is emotionally moving. It is encouraging in nature. It generates a passion to work, in your favor. Your subordinates or team members whom you lead are obsessed by your ideas. They behave zealously towards ensuring that your idea is a huge success. It is sort of crazy behavior - all to make your idea succeed. THAT is wielding soft power over your colleagues and subordinates.

Now let us look at the scenario from the other side - a subordinate's point of view. How would we feel working for such an individual? A senior or boss who sweetly, lovingly, cajoles us towards fulfillment of a particular plan which would ensure success of the Organizational objectives. A person who also ensures giving us due credit for every input we contribute with, be it hard work, an original idea, for each and every moment that we zealously work at our jobs - something that we are anyway supposed to do - yet we are acknowledged for every small and big input of ours.

Wouldn't it feel brilliant? Our hearts would be dazzling and our souls shining. Not only would these positive attributes convert into success and prosperity monetarily, it would make us feeling wholesome and complete. It would feel so nice to be acknowledged in being a part of and one of the reasons of the success story. The ownership of the success would feel exhilarating.

That is the dazzle that 'Soft Power' holds - not only for the person who wields it but also to the person who follows in the light of Soft Power. It is a win-win situation for all. And because of the extremely positive and strong energy, the manifestation of thoughts is all the more faster, stronger and permanent.

Chapter 4

Hard Power Vs Soft Power

Let us now take a look at the traditional, most used and according to many, an extremely effective way of managing through the use of Hard Power. Some swear by its efficacy. Some follow the adage - 'The person above you is GOD and the one below you is a DOG'.

The chief feature exhibited by managers who brandish Hard Power is the 'hire and fire' or the 'promote-demote' methods. Every order is laced with a threat of superiority by which fear is induced to ensure completion of work. You would find such managers very easily usurping the credits which are due to subordinates too. Frustration and other such negative feelings are what rise in the subordinates' minds and one soon has run-of-the-mill kind of outputs.

Managers using this style of functioning are many, but such managers do not metamorphose into leaders. In fact they, due to the Law of Attraction and the Law of Karma, bear the brunt of such negativities in different ways in their lives. Exceptions though are not ruled out. But exceptions do not make the rule.

'Leaders' on the other hand across the globe, are individuals who wield tremendous Soft Power. Not only are they the most successful, they are the most long-term effective too.

From here on, we would take up the attributes which successfully evolve team-leaders and managers into successful managers and gradually into mentors and leaders. Prior to this we shall reveal the Principles of Manifesting Thoughts which use the power of the subconscious mind to manifest and attract situations. The understanding of these Principles would need the introduction to *Thought Forms*. It would then be easy to understand and synergize with each attribute thought management techniques which would guide in speedy manifestations.

Chapter 5

The World of Thought Forms

Before we go ahead with Soft Power Management, we will explain a bit about Thought Forms and the Principles of Manifesting Thoughts. Some portions of this chapter have been taken from the author's book 'Manifesting Thoughts Effortlessly'.

Whatever we see in the Physical World has a FORM – Buildings, Cars, Humans, Computers, etc.... Our identification of people or objects is by their forms.

But is there anything in this world which is without a form? Something, which we cannot see with the naked eye but only experience? Yes, there very much is - They are 'Thoughts & Feelings'. Every Thought, every Feeling is a Living Entity. It has Life Energy &

has a Form.

A question which naturally comes to mind after reading this strange concept is "Can we <u>see</u> these Thought Forms?" The answer most definitely is "Yes, but only people who have developed their faculty of Clairvoyance can". Now what is Clairvoyance or who is a Clairvoyant? Well, Clairvoyants can read auras or see "etheric bodies" or "energy bodies". Next another question which comes to mind - What is an 'aura' or 'etheric body'?

Well, as human beings we have energy within us. If we didn't, we wouldn't be able to move about or do any of the hundreds of things we can do with our bodies. Now, this energy is not just in the muscles of arms and legs but is very much a part of each and every cell of our body. And why only the body, this "energy" is within each cell, within our body and also extends till outside the body. This energy portion which 'juts' out of the body is known as "Aura". The aura has physical, emotional and mental attributes.

Now just because you are reading this in this book, why should you believe it? As rational humans we believe what we see, not just what we read. Right? Then, how do we see an aura, if as written previously, only Clairvoyants can? As per general understanding, Clairvoyants are some hocus focus people, or voodoo related beings or humans who meditate a lot or something like that.... As a 'normal' human being it is only natural to believe what you see and not just what you are being told that someone else can see, but you can't.

So let's see, how do we make you understand a concept which you may read but can't see. Well simple, we make you see it. How? By photographing it. Simple. Aura or energies can be photographed by the use of 'Kirlian Photography'. Semyon Kirlian in 1939 was the first to photograph the aura – of humans, leaves, coins.... Therefore, not only humans and animals but everything including plants and inanimate objects like metals has energy! In fact everything, whether we can see it or not, whether it can be felt only or heard only, is made up of energy. Thought forms too are made up of energy. Just that their characteristics vary.

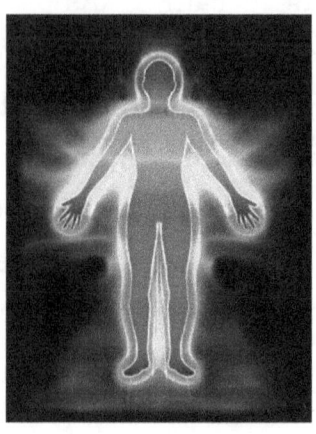

Clairvoyants are able to 'see' and 'read' the aura or the energy in a human being, in a particular area, in a house of office space, in relations between two humans.... The list is endless. Is there a separate language to read these energies which can be learnt? No, this is something that cannot be learnt but 'develops' in people who are interested in this subject.

Regular meditation also ensures development of this faculty. The energy which has life in it, is seen as pulsating. This pulsation may also be referred to as having a 'frequency'. The higher & stronger the frequency, the higher or better or stronger energy.

The aura of human beings has energy centers or 'chakras', which again have physical, emotional and mental attributes. These chakras are in constant movement removing negative, used up energy and producing fresh and positive energy in the body. The work of the energy centers is to circulate energy throughout the body. The energy produced by the chakras is colored, which have certain , emotional and mental attributes too. We shall not dwell into the technical aspect of the chakras in this book, but the author shall explain the meaning and attributes as and when required in the context of the Law of Attraction.

For regular people like us, to be able to understand this concept, let us do a simple 1 second experiment – The moment you hear the word "Car", what comes to mind – an image of a "Car", right? Now that is a "Thought form of a Car". So put simply, a thought form looks like how your thought feels like. Just that the Thought Forms are in "Images". A feeling of anger, love, happiness, house, and success would have corresponding Forms.

Now, let's come to what characteristics thought forms have?

The *characteristics of Thought forms* are:

• It has a <u>Form</u> – known as "Thought Form"

• It has <u>Life Energy</u> in it

• It has the capacity to <u>move</u> about

• It has the capacity to <u>embed</u> itself

• It has the capacity to <u>grow</u> like a living entity

Having explained the first two in the paragraphs above, let us come to the third characteristic – 'The capacity to move about'. Some times while walking on the road (esp. this is more often felt by ladies), it is felt that there is something which disturbs us suddenly, and we move our heads to see someone inappropriately staring at us. What happens is that the person staring, has released a particular thought form, which does not 'feel' good and has travelled from his aura to our aura and the moment it touches our aura we are able to 'feel' the discomforting thought form. Conversely when we enter a room of people who are known to us and are favorable in their approach to us, we feel nice and pleasant. This is due to the thought forms and feelings of love or liking which have travelled from their aura to our aura and hence we 'feel' the niceness.

The fourth characteristic is – 'The capacity to *embed* itself'. Often when we hear a tune which we like, we hum the same all day. Or if some unfavorable incident spoils our mood, we feel low the whole day, unless something happens to the contrary. In the first case the pleasurable thoughts & feelings associated with the song are what have 'embedded' in our aura and hence we are humming the same the whole day. Let us take another case, of an upset mood - the thought forms of uneasiness of the unfavorable incident have embedded in our aura and we feel upset the whole day & hence feel low. This embedding of the negative form is like a blood-sucker and sucks out the energy from our auras and hence we keep on feeling low.

The fifth characteristic is about 'growing like a living entity'. Let us take an example - When we hear of an epidemic like dengue or cholera or any such disease which we are scared of suffering, the same begins with information from a either the newspaper or a TV channel. But this thought form of the fear of the disease, keeps on getting bigger and bigger and soon we hear many in the streets also discussing it. Now this thought form which was communicated to us through the TV channel, embedded in our aura and due to the fear emotion associated with the disease this thought form kept on being replenished with energy and kept on growing bigger and bigger. Had this thought form been nipped in the bud, the same would not have 'grown' into an epidemic. The thought form of the disease was brought into the experience of a lot of lives and they had to physically & mentally suffer the same.

Chapter 6

The Principles of

'Manifesting Thoughts'

1.   The Law of Attraction states that whatever your dominant/ habitual/ believed thoughts are, you will attract similar experiences into your life. "Energy follows thought".

2.   Thought forms laced with any particular emotion, manifest in the hue of the emotion. Thoughts with positive emotions beget positive manifestation and vice versa.

3. As thought forms embed and grow, whatever thoughts are produced by our conscious mind, verily move between our Conscious and Subconscious. This is the reason our personalities reflect our thoughts. Our personalities are a reflection of our

Subconscious.

4. The Universal Consciousness which encompasses all is the strongest, vastest, and purest form of energy known. It is present in and controls all activities, including the movement of galaxies. All wisdom, knowledge, inventions, prosperity, etc. are contained in it.

Our Subconscious is a part of the Universal Consciousness. It is the inter-connect for our Conscious mind and is also the storehouse of habits, memory and karmic records.

5. Thoughts created in the Conscious mind are realized for us *from* the Universal Consciousness, *by* our Subconscious. The three Consciousnesses are like one egg inside another, yet inside another, with the Universal Consciousness being like the outer-most and biggest egg.

6. One good deed begets ten more and similarly one bad deed begets ten more. Karmic manifestations are magnified in

nature. Be aware and be responsible of your karma.

7. Whatever thoughts laced with emotions and beliefs are created by our Conscious mind, our Subconscious begets similar magnified experiences from the Universal Consciousness. This is Manifestation of Thought.

Chapter 7

Your demeanor and personality

Humans are visual beings. It is said a picture is worth a thousand words. This is so because we retain information in our subconscious in the form of images. This is already explained in the chapter on 'Thought Forms'.

Remember, how your colleagues, seniors, subordinates or business contacts view you as an individual or professional, is how you project so. Any individual is known by his or her behavior and personality. The more amiable the same, the more 'likeability' factor it contains. We all like to touch a smooth surface, not a rough one - in the same way a smooth demeanor is what helps you to 'be liked' by others. Smoothness and polish are what shine brightest in a personality. Now let us take a small peek into what makes up a 'smooth and polished' personality.

In childhood, our family, our schooling, our peers and friends are whom we learn from. As we grow up, based on those young age impressions, we develop likes, dislikes and views on various aspects of life. These thoughts, views and experiences are what go into molding our personalities. The sense of what is right and what is wrong develops and is seen in perspective of people around us. With age and experience we mature. The same is reflected in our demeanor and personality.

Our personality is one of the strongest attributes of Soft Power we may wield in life and our professions. A leader or manager's personality must be smooth to the feel, but strong as a bull. It must shine like a diamond, but not hurt the eyes. Mesmerizing must be the approach, but not to over-awe. The vision should be that of a King, which focuses on prosperity and well being for the entire kingdom, not only for filling of one's own coffers. It necessarily must be all encompassing. It must flow like a river, never stagnating and must nourish civilizations along its banks.

Such thoughts as mentioned above, when ingrained in the subconscious, are what bring smoothness and polish to the personality. 'Being smooth to the feel' is important so that your subordinates and colleagues feel at ease being and working with you. The comfortability factor plays a big role in acceptance of a personality.

Being 'strong as a bull' is an attribute which lends credence to the fact that the person is not easily swayed, week-kneed and holds his ground in difficult or unfavorable circumstances too. For people around it is important to believe in your character, which must be strong. Your 'dependability factor' is greatly enhanced by this attribute. Do not read this as being obstinate, but being strong and upholding one's virtues.

'Shining like a diamond' denotes brightness. Brightness of knowledge, of ideas, of wisdom. In short it denotes 'brilliance'. Brilliance comes not only from knowledge but from experimentation and experience. As a team leader or manager, your knowledge about your product or work must be thorough. You must know of your subject like the back of your hand. And the most important part of knowing your subject is in the implementation of the same. Not the traditional type of implementation (that is so predictable) but innovative ideas played out thoroughly in your mind, along with their pros and cons. A lot of people do come up with brilliant ideas, but they are unable to show it the light of day. Caged brilliance is no brilliance. If it does not benefit, it means nothing. It must be executed and implemented. Strive for this brilliance and you would find your own personality shining all the more from within.

Have you had the wonderful luck of

working with a great leader? If you have, you would have observed how even their small nuances are etched in your memory, how their ideas have molded your own thinking, how their facial expressions play out in front of you when you close your eyes. That is being mesmerized. Not only are the physical attributes and styles of behavior outwardly remembered, the ideas, thoughts and visions of such personalities are deeply ingrained in our own thinking.

The outward behavior, subtle nuances, use of language, the delivery of words in how you wish to convey them, all are part of your demeanor. As a leader, remember you are subject to being observed through a magnifying glass. Hence work on these attributes. For the expressions and nuances part, act out in front of the mirror. Remove weaknesses or ungainly nuances which may have unknowingly crept into your behavior. Strengthen and better styles that look pleasing to the eye as well as truly bring out your uniqueness.

Your voice, your style of expression, your pitch, and your pronunciations may be recorded and played back for you to analyze. With a neutral point of view critically go through it. Thereafter further enhance your strengths and weed out the weaknesses (you may also refer to the author's book 'Manifesting Impressive Public Speaking and Presentation Skills'). Your voice, the choice and delivery of words are what go a long way to be remembered by people as part of your demeanor and personality. Hence work on making it powerful, yet pleasing.

Your sense of dressing too plays an important part in the projection of your internal likes, choices and style. The choice of clothes reflects the inner state of mind too, to a large extent. If your emotional and mental state is happy and confident it would reflect on your choice of clothing. Whether you are flamboyant or subtle, strong willed or mentally apologetic, confident or confused, remember your outer state and choice of clothes reflect the inner personality. Hence inwardly, make subtle shifts in your thought process, so that outwardly it would reflect in your demeanor and dressing. If you are not the fashion-wise type of individual, follow the thumb rule of dressing conservatively and as per occasion.

Let's now talk about the attribute of having the Vision of a King. Vision is long term in nature as well as it is like having a 30000 feet view from above of various perspectives. Just like a kingdom needs to be planned out, each and every aspect worked out for smooth running, securing it from all sides, ensuring health, education, prosperity for all, similarly a leader or a manager needs to work out his or her vision. What is needed is the collating of many short and long term goals intertwining each other. Each small goal has to be conquered through relative plans and the completion of many such small goals help manifest the vision. To be able to manifest your vision, you would need your colleagues and subordinates to believe in your vision and work as a team, taking responsibilities of making a success various small plans and achieving these goals. Now earning their faith in your vision is the biggest challenge.

Once again there are two approaches - (A) Handing the plans down to them to implement, which is the traditional method and (B) Making their beliefs one with your belief and vision. When your belief appeals to their heart that is when the fructifying and manifesting of your vision begins. That is when with an infected enthusiasm do they start giving it their all. That is when they start living your dream, your vision. But how does this happen? And when does this happen? That is the big question.

Simply put, this happens when you have won them over with your ideas, with your behavior, with your personality; in short your brilliance. An individual's biggest contribution comes when he feels being 'part' of the idea.

Deliberately look for constructive and creative criticism from them for your ideas. This will help in further refinement of your ideas and ensure success. In the subordinates minds and hearts, it will highlight self-worth and self-respect. They will also have the feeling of 'being heard', which is a major point of disappointment in many people. Only then will they feel being 'a part of' the vision. Only then will they give it their 100% to make your vision a reality. On your part, ensure that as per plan and as per allocation of responsibilities, you guide, mould and nurture them towards the fulfillment of your vision. This is when you graduate from being a manager to a leader and a visionary.

In the paragraph above the attribute of nurturing is mentioned. A few paragraphs before the metaphor of the river was provided which nurtured civilizations on its shores. This nurturing is the biggest selfless service you can do towards mankind. An individual normally nurtures his or her own child. All the best amenities as per one's capacity are provided to the child. The heart grows big with happiness and contentment on the child's success and achievements. Nurturing is the biggest attribute provided to mankind, where selfless service is given. Endeavour to nurture your subordinates. Share with them your knowledge and guidance; correct and guide them where wrong. Be benevolent in your approach. That is when you will have their unconditional love and trust. That is when they will be indebted to you for life. That is when you metamorphose from a manager to a mentor. That is your real success and the highest attribute to attain, which shall stay with you for life - to be a mentor to others.

Chapter 8

Mentor yourself first

The dictionary meaning of 'Mentor' is - a wise and trusted senior. The chief attributes of a mentor are experience, patience, wisdom and trust. As a manager or team leader, you already have a certain amount of knowledge and experience about your job, that's why you are in the position of a manager. But, being in that position is not the be-all and end-all of life. You need to progress in life and career. The biggest gift you can give yourself is bettering your own self first, every single day. Remember, your biggest competitor is no one from outside, but your own self. You need to compete with your yesterday's achievement and better it today. There can be no two ways about this. And there can be no let up on this, every single day of your life.

Be it the bettering of yesterday's sales figures, or bettering of the knowledge levels, or bettering of relationships, or bettering of anything in your life and career which is important to you. Each step of betterment comes with application and experience and each such step is a direction in amassing wisdom.

Begin with metamorphosing your own thoughts and attitude from being a manager to being a mentor. Work actively in this direction by guiding others. Every solution that you come up with your experience to a subordinate's problem, you are taking a step in this direction. Every time you guide and nurture a subordinate, by the Principles of Manifesting Thoughts', you are strengthening the thought form of mentorship and more knowledge will be attracted towards you to enrich you. Every step you take in helping, guiding, and nurturing also attracts the emotion of trust towards you.

Patience, as mentioned before, is one of

the attributes of a mentor. Subordinates, due to lesser experience and knowledge, many a times are unable to fathom the importance and depth of the guidance they receive from their mentors. At such times it upon you, the mentor, to keep one's cool as well as be patient and persevering in your approach. The end result you foresee for your subordinate is most important. Do not lose focus of this, as it will help you to persevere.

Seniors in the Organization too are on the lookout for individuals who have such attributes of mentorship. It is important for them too, to elevate such individuals who have the talent of being mentors and then gradually leaders. Then only is Organizational continuity maintained. It is because of such forward thinking that Organizations grow from strength to strength and prosper and mature with time.

Chapter 9

Personal Equity

As humans, one of the biggest bonding factors that we see from early childhood is trust. Trust, that we as small kids have on our parents that they would protect us from all harm. Trust that we have on our favorite uncle for guiding and standing by us. Trust, that we have on our friends, that our secrets would be safe with them. Trust on our lover, who will never betray us. Trust on our husband or wife for being there for us in good times and bad. Trust on our colleagues that they would be with us in every step.

Trust or faith is what keeps the whole world going. And it is this trust that we need to understand is our strongest forte in the field of managing. Trust that we earn from our colleague, subordinates and seniors for ourselves. Under no circumstances should this trust be broken, comes hell or high waters. The word 'trust' may also be coined as 'personal equity'.

Needless to say, trust or personal equity is something that is built in a sustained manner over a period of time. It is following the truth, no matter what comes in our way. It is ensuring that we strive to fulfill every commitment; every word which comes out of our mouth is the truth and not mixed with double meaning words which hoodwink people; our thoughts reflect care and understanding and we ensure that no harm befalls others who are with us; we show strong determination and character even in the face of untoward pressures and do not budge from our commitments.

Personal equity comes with a loyal following only to people who are loyal to others. This is a very strong statement and rock-solid true.

Chapter 10

Personal behavior

A person is remembered, forgotten, loved or despised because of his or her behavior. The real introduction to an individual's personality is through his or her behavior. It wouldn't be an exaggeration to say that it is our behavior which projects our emotional and mental states of being.

As a leader of your team, as explained before, each and every miniscule nuance of yours is as if being observed with a magnifying glass. Hence not only to be accepted in the correct light, but to ensure that the best projection of your own personality comes forth, so that the subordinates may learn from you, ensure that your personal behavior must be highly refined.

It is natural to be angered about a mistake, it is natural to be frustrated over a nagging problem, it is natural to fear the loss of a tender enquiry or not being able to meet the deadline of a particular job. After all you are human. But how elegantly and with peace in your mind do you handle the situation, depends totally on you. The 'Meditation on Gold' has been advised in this book. Take help of this meditation or any other meditation that you may be aware of, but ensure you set aside even if just 10-15 minutes a day for the same. With regular meditation, not only emotionally are you strengthened to withstand various upheavals that may present themselves before you on a day to day basis, mentally too you would be strengthened to obtain clear and discerning thinking capabilities. You would be surprised with the ease, calm and maturity you handle untoward situations. Not all situations can go according to your likings, but what you would possess is the ability to face the same with élan.

When the mind is calm and the emotions in control, your facial expressions and body language too help calm the nerves of others around you. And help in clear understanding of the situation as well as of the handling of the same.

Chapter 11

Walk the talk

The one big pro and the one big con (whichever way you wish to take it), when you are in a position of power or in the limelight, is that each and every nuance of yours is as if seen with a magnifying glass - every word which comes out of your mouth, every decision you take, your moods, your clothes, your likes, your dislikes, what you eat, when you eat, how long you take in the wash room... Like it or not, everything about you. Sounds like more of an excerpt of some film actor being followed by fans or the paparazzi... Right?

Any position which entails followers (not only fans) is something like this only. You as the manager, are keenly followed by subordinates and in turn you in the role of subordinate to the CEO, Directors and other such seniors, follow them keenly. It is human nature, to look up to someone and learn. The person who is being followed by others or in other words is a leader in his given area, is hence naturally 'observed' by others. Hence it becomes very important for the leader to not send out wrong signals. 'Responsible' actions are a must, as the leader's actions are followed and duplicated. The fans of an actor wear clothes of the same style or get their hair styled to emulate. The subordinates in an Organization on the other hand emulate decision making processes, behavior, pattern of expenses, revenue generating ideas and various day to day managerial techniques and processes. Hence you as a leader to a certain group must exhibit responsible actions as well as examples you wish to set for others. In simple terms, you need to 'walk the talk'.

If you wish your subordinates to put in an extra four hours of work, ensure you put in at least five hours. If you wish to save on the electricity costs of your office, ensure you switch off the AC and lights etc of your chamber before you leave. If you wish to have transparency in dealings with suppliers, ensure you follow and show the same. If you want your sales force to make 15 to 20 visits a day, go out for a week into the market and make 20 to 25 visits a day. It must be 'seen' by the subordinates. And it must be seen in the 'hue' you wish it to be emulated in. That is important and that is the reason of being seen as having 'responsible' behavior.

You as a leader have to imbibe and execute with this very important tool and this very important Soft Power in being able to guide your team in the direction you know will fulfill Organizational goals.

Chapter 12

Communication channels

One big attribute that many managers fail to give importance to is keeping communication channels open with and within their subordinates and team. Whenever and wherever this happens, the flow of energy is blocked. Imagine sitting in an air-tight glass cubicle. As because there is no ventilation, after a certain amount of time, you would feel choked. That is exactly what happens when communication channels are not open - choking occurs.

Communication could take any shape - formal business communication, general communication of ideas, and personal communication as in human caring. Of these three, the most important communication which gives a strong base is personal communication. We shall explain why.

Humans are egoistic by nature. Most relationship issues, you would observe, are because of this one negative trait in us. We very conveniently name such egoistic behavior as 'misunderstandings' as we don't wish to be identified with this negative trait.

Relationship issues based on egoism may occur in any relationship - between lovers, between husband and wife, between friends, between siblings, between father and son, between mother and daughter, between co-students, between colleagues, between seniors and juniors in an office environment. It could rear its ugly head anywhere because the human psychology and nature is so.

As a manager or team leader you need to be careful that because of this psychological attribute, the very first thing that gets affected is the Communication between the individuals. That is choking in nature.

When open communication between team

members or colleagues occurs, you would see fresh ideas, enthusiastic approaches, camaraderie, a do-or-die feeling for others is common. Free exchange of thoughts enriches the thought forms all the more and you would find your team coming up with award winning ideas and performances.

Again when open communication between seniors and juniors occur, a cross-flow of fresh and mature thought forms bring out the best in both. Not only is there free circulation of energy, the free undaunted circulation of thoughts helps each one excel. There is a feeling of completeness, of lightness.

As a manager if you could ensure 'open communication' between your team members, between yourself and your subordinates, between yourself and your seniors, you would observe a 'collective rising' of business and personal success levels. Ensure you iron out the very first 'crease' you see in any relationship. Talk it out with people. Clear their doubts. Pacify nerves. Do whatever you need to do depending on the situation, but nip it in the bud itself. Ensure open, clean and well-lubricated communication channels.

Chapter 13

Turn your promises into reality

Every word spoken by a senior is hung on to by subordinates. For them these words are full of meaning. They would like to trust their senior. They would like to believe in him or her.

Never ever use words loosely. Whatever you say must be pregnant with meaning and commitment. Your words generate expectations and fulfilling them is your responsibility. This fulfilling of your responsibility, of actualizing your words and promises helps raise your personal worth.

A lot many seniors are not respected by their colleagues and subordinates because they do not keep their word. Unfulfilled promises leave a bad taste in the mouth. One does work for such a senior because it is part of one's job, but the feeling of loyalty or the feeling of giving one's all to make such a senior's idea successful, like one's own, would never be there. Such seniors are in fact seen with apprehension and by the subordinates. There is a general sense of disbelief. With such thought forms moving about in the Organization, the manifestation of ideas too is laden with negativities. That is something which is a must-avoid.

Ensure that before you use words, you have carefully thought and worked out the pros and cons. If you are yourself not sure, be clear in your communication. Provide the realistic aspect to your team, subordinates and colleagues. Appeal to them to stand by you in removing the cons. Only your truthful explanation will ensure you are ably supported in fulfilling your commitments.

Chapter 14

Collaborative approach to success

'A captain is as good as his Team'. This is a phrase normally found in sports. A team leader may have the best of ideas, the best of knowledge about his job, but till the wisdom of the collaborative approach is not there, he or she cannot move on from being an able leader to a great leader. That is the power of collaboration or team-work.

A manager's main job is to show direction, plan and coordinate the various diverse functions needed to reach the goal and ensure a cohesive and collaborative movement of energy towards making the Organizational goal a success.

The human element in a plan is the most important as well as the most complex aspect and is such a major ingredient that no success is possible without the whole-hearted inputs only a human being can bring into success. And it is this human aspect which builds team spirit. The feeling of belonging and being a member of a team, in whichever position as well as the feeling of responsibility and collaboratively sharing for collective success, is your most important job as well as challenge.

As mentioned before, humans are the most complex aspect of a plan. It is this complex aspect that one needs to work on and work with. Egos, feelings, likes, dislikes, strengths, weaknesses and many more attributes and emotions are what make up an attitude within a human being. There is no fixed formula that can be ever written, but the more humane your approach, the more understanding would you have of the human psyche. Molding and motivating individually is what you would need to do, to be able to fine tune the process towards success in a collective goal. Every individual's need is different and every individual's need would have to be addressed differently. Some need to be cajoled, some need to be reminded of their inner or core strengths, some need to be guided in their thought process; every individual's handling would be different. This would come from experience of the humane kind and not so much from books.

The feeling of camaraderie is perhaps one of the most important aspects you would need to build into the subconscious of your individual team members. Using the Manifesting Thoughts Principles, bring about radical changes in the experiences you wish to draw into your own and your team's psyche. There are a lot of team building exercises prescribed by various people. How many people have you seen actually living the same after the training module is over? Team building is not a 9 to 5 job. It is a 24 hour job. As a manager you need to involve your team members in consciously teaming up for small and big chores - in office as well as their personal lives. This repeated enactment of small plans would ensure a habit of team work which settles in the subconscious. Once the same is part of the subconscious, your work becomes all the easier and bigger plans can be smoothly worked out.

Chapter 15

Do not micro-manage

A lot of people have it in them of not having faith on anyone other than themselves. For some reason they feel that no one other than themselves can be fully entrusted a particular job and in the event of them delegating a job, their continuous interference ensures that the job is not done properly as per the delegated person's best of abilities. Simply put, this is nagging in its purest form.

As a manager when you delegate a particular job, you do so knowing the abilities of an individual. But apart from abilities which are visible, there are many more latent abilities that every individual possesses. When given a task and 100% freedom to execute a task, you would be surprised to see a lot of innovative ways and solutions people come up with. This is because every individual is unique. We as human society prefer conditioning the brain of others, hence look for solutions that we ourselves identify with. This is also so because it is within our 'comfort zone'. Such an approach is not only run-of-the-mill kind, it is stagnating and defeating in nature.

When we hire a person for a particular job, we already have prefixed ideas as to what jobs a person in that position can do or is supposed to do. Everything is pre-conceived in our own minds. Mentally we have drawn boundaries of responsibility, ability, response and output. We even expect a person to reply or revert in a particular manner. That is damaging. That is restricting the person as well as us.

Instead use Soft Power. Give the work/ project to the individual and ask him or her to find a solution or complete it within the shortest possible time. In most cases you will be surprised of receiving never thought before innovative solutions. And in case you find that the person is not able to solve or complete it, you too would have something to realize - (A) Analyze whether the person is good enough for the particular job; (B) Check for inherent flaws in the particular job/ project. If the person is not correct for the particular job, without wasting further time you would be able to take corrective measures. And if the particular job or project has inherent flaws, you know what to do about it.

From the viewpoint of the subordinate, when the senior allots a job and along with it the freedom to go about it in his or her own way, not only do the creative juices flow, there is an additional feeling of responsibility to live up to the trust. This feeling of being entrusted with the work is a great game-changer. Even subordinates, who may not take naturally to you, would be mentally and emotionally inclined thereafter. The project would have undivided attention, the best innovative thought forms flow, you have unique fresh energy which is infective and invigorative to others too. And at the end of a successful project, ensure you give the due and necessary credits.

As a manager you may have various departments to work with and your main work is to ensure smooth workings and coordination between them. Create the culture amongst the various Head-of-Departments to also outline the work required within the time frame and give the necessary freedom to complete the jobs. Keep an eye only on a macro level to guide where wrong. Micromanaging not only takes away too much time, it is interfering in nature. Use this time and energy for thinking big - Bigger ideas, newer approaches and techniques of bettering productivity, innovating procedures, etc., and by the Principle of Manifesting Thoughts, you and your Head-of-Departments would attract to yourself and your Organization things much bigger than you ever imagined.

Chapter 16

Innovative ideas

As a manager or a leader of your team a very important, healthy and vision-forming exercise that must be undertaken is 'innovating ideas'. Humans have this psychology to be ensconced in their comfort zones, which results in run-of-the-mill kind of outputs. Ensure your team and subordinates are not part of such a rut.

To have a vibrant team, a very important role you must play is of pushing for out-of-the-box ideas and new ways to do the same old job. Every time you push for innovative thinking to better the present way of working, as per the Principle of Manifesting Thoughts, you are ensuring that the knowledge and wisdom of the subconscious is being tapped into. Fresh flow of ideas would result.

Learning has no age and no boundaries. When you push and support your team to think of innovative solutions, you would be surprised as to so many new things you too would learn from them. The next step, due to your experience and maturity would be of 'constructive feedback'. Critically examine every new idea, check out the pros and cons, and put it to test selectively, guide the subordinate as to the strengths and weaknesses of the idea. Ensure your body language as well as words are positive. At times you may get frustrated with some individual, but it should not reflect on your face. Such individuals are slow starters; ensure you keep on persevering and doing your job as a mentor. Correct constructively in the sense that you guide them towards the correct path as well as ensure that the individual is not demoralized with failure.

Where the leader of a team propagates innovative thinking, it has tell-tale signs of a healthy team. The free and fresh flow of thought forms ensures trust as well as gratitude towards the senior. With innovative ideas and solutions being thought of, the short-term as well as long-term vision of the Organization gets a boost. It is only Teams and Organizations which constantly keep on innovating and re-innovating small and big processes, which grow on to be world leaders in their particular industry. Forward thinking approach results, which also becomes the benchmark for others.

Chapter 17

Encompassing Prosperity

The objective of any business is to make profit. Being the part of an Organization and holding a responsible position, it not only is your job to ensure profit or value addition to the work, it is important that you set a base for continuous prosperity.

Now prosperity can never be long-running if the same does not ensure prosperity for all. As per the Principle of Manifesting Thoughts, what thought forms you spread, you receive a magnified version of the same back in your experience. Hence, the introduction of the concept 'Encompassing Prosperity' here.

While you work towards prosperity for yourself, you must necessarily think of prosperity for the person or Organization you are doing business with also. The idea should never be to fleece someone else for your own prosperity. If so be the case, you may have a winning situation in your hands for once only, definitely not in the long term. Such success is not part of a larger canvas, but constricted thoughts would bring experiences to you, where you would be at the receiving end in future, not necessarily in the same way.

Win-Win is an attitude which is lodged in the subconscious. It looks at prosperity for all, with happiness. Envy or deceit does not play a role here. When you are looking at profit for your own Organization, you must necessarily look for prosperity of the Companies you are dealing with too, who may be with you in the form of vendors or clients. When you look at value addition, you must look at it for all concerned. Do not worry that there may be something less for you. Prosperity is a mind-set. The Universal Consciousness, of which your Subconscious is a part, is Prosperity Unlimited. Once this attitude sets in and lodges in your subconscious, you will experience what is also known as 'good luck' because you would be, by default, tapping into this *Unlimited Universal Prosperity* as an attitude. Hence always think Win-Win and *Encompassing Prosperity* and broaden your mental view to include all.

Chapter 18

Practice Humility

There is a saying in the Hindi language which states that 'The more a tree is laden with fruits, the more it bends towards the ground'. Humility is the antonym of arrogance. Humility comes from the supreme confidence of knowledge. A confident and knowledgeable person does not need to show high airs. Confidence without humility is arrogance.

Have you had the opportunity to listen to extremely successful personalities? A striking feature is the humility with which they talk. It is this humility which is appalling as well as disarming. This characteristic needs to be imbibed in the subconscious too, if one wishes to be truly successful.

This attribute of humility opens closed doors as well as closed and guarded personalities; and ensures love and respect for the person practicing it. Humility, it is said is like Godliness. Whichever faith or religion you may belong to, this is one philosophy that transcend all and is common to all. Even if you are an atheist, it does not matter; what matters is that you understand how deep and vast humility is, like an ocean, surrounding all.

With the attribute of humility comes peace within. With peace comes stillness. With stillness comes the power of discernment. With discernment comes the understanding and wisdom to handle all situations in profession and life.

When you practice humility, you would experience, how your seniors, colleagues, subordinates, business friends and people you deal with, have belief in your words; how they look up to you; how they would love to be near you and prefer working with you. This is Soft

Power which strengthens the soul all the more - in business, at work, in family and in life.

Humility should never be mistaken for weakness. Neither should you ever consider such a thought nor should your body language project so. Humility is a state of mind and a state of being which results from knowledge and wisdom of understanding the truth. In fact a humble person is an extremely strong person emotionally and mentally and is non-wavering in his or her approach and understanding. It is like being rock solid inside with a soft exterior. A humble personality is so because it recognizes that knowledge and wisdom are blessings. Very few are thus blessed and the feeling of gratitude by being humble ensures all the more that your subconscious draws in magnified blessings of more knowledge and wisdom from the Universal Consciousness.

Conversely a haughty, proud and arrogant person in the vanity if knowledge that he or she may have gained, constrict and close themselves to such further knowledge and subsequent wisdom.

Chapter 19

Dignified Approach

A dignified approach to life comes from extensive experience. The élan with which one conducts oneself is a reflection of one's inner self - the thought process, the emotional make-up and the experience. The inner self draws its power from the Subconscious mind. Some thinkers also consider the two to be conjoined.

Let us expand on the word 'Dignity'. Dignity corresponds to excellence - in thoughts and deeds. It is the non-compromising attitude of not stopping short and leaving no stone unturned to achieve excellence in whatever one does. It also denotes the strength of character, of not bowing down to outside pressure and of doing the 'right' thing.

Dignity reeks of culture, nobility, decency and grace in handling not only major issues at profession or life but also comparatively day to day mundane work. The behavioral handling does not change as per the size or importance of the issue, but is constantly non-compromising. For example you do not behave in a dignified manner only when you are pointing out the mistake of a senior; but also act in a dignified manner and not 'bark' at a subordinate's mistake. Your behavior should not change in such different situations.

A dignified approach comes when you respect your own self, when you not only follow ideals, you by example create them. It comes from a sense of morality. It comes from the basis of respecting others as humans. Respect begets respect and the more you exhibit it towards others, as per the Principle of Manifesting Thoughts you are in a much better position to receive a magnified reflection of the same.

Always treat others to your own standards

of dignity. When you do this, you not only raise the bar, you ensure an environment for yourself and others to be in such an elated state.

Chapter 20

Moral authority

How many of us remember the stories and lessons learnt at Morals class when we were in school? Not many of us, we are sure. But then, we don't necessarily need to remember those stories; we need to imbibe the lessons in our subconscious.

Now imagine being with someone you consider being a moral authority. It could be a friend, a senior, a relative or the priest. How nicely comfortable it would feel in such a person's presence. The comfortability factor comes from the feeling that one is safe in such a person's presence. Such a person would do no harm to us. It is only human to be concerned about one's safety and comfort. In fact one 'looks upon' such a personality which exudes moral authority.

As a team leader or manager, the respect that you beget is also due to the morality you indulge with, in your job. Transparency in dealings, professionally non-violent and non-vindictive stands, ensuring maintaining of Organizational ethos even at the cost of personal affect; these are but a few of the activities that one exhibits at work. And these matter to a large and deep extent.

A long term vision is expounded when one touches the psychological 'nerve' of an individual, wherein the emotions and the ethical mind is impressed with behavior one sees and experiences. The important attributes of a person exuding moral authority are if he or she possesses ethicality, honesty, decency, gentleness, integrity, justice and principles. Such an individual is seen as an ideal to be looked up to.

When you the team leader are able to generate such wonder and awe, you are able to generate a 'fan-following'. It is when you are viewed as having high moral authority that you appeal to the higher emotions of your subordinates and colleagues. It is then that you are able to lead your 'pack' in the higher interests of the Organization. It is also then that your inputs are magnified and noticed by your higher-ups; and you are viewed for larger roles in the Organization.

Therefore ensure that your personality and your subconscious is, like in the process of osmosis, blended in with the attributes of strong and smooth moral character and therefore authority.

Chapter 21

'Listening to'

Most of us love to talk, don't we? In fact communication would not happen if we did not express our thoughts. But communication has two sides - the person expressing thoughts and the person listening to.

As a manager or team leader, a major amount of time is consumed telling people what and how to do. That's the job, right? But a very important aspect which is missed by many a senior, is of listening to subordinates.

Every individual feels nice being listened to. It gives a feeling that 'yes, my thoughts and feelings are important'. It gives a boost to one's self esteem. It provides fillip to the feeling of responsibility to do one's job better. On an internal plane, it gives a sense of belonging, a sense of being.

From yours, the managers view point, when you are inclined to and do provide the time and effort to listen, you are non-verbally conveying that you care for the individual and that his or her thoughts and opinions matter to you. Also, when you listen avidly you are able to judge the subordinate on these counts - the feeling of responsibility towards the job, the intellectual level, the understanding and deciphering abilities of the individual. When a person talks to you, he or she is opening up their personalities to you. Hence 'listening to' is a hugely important aspect which would help in carrying out your job as a manager in a most effective way.

Chapter 22

Smile

For some reason the managerial position is identified with seriousness. It is commonly expected and seen that people in such positions rarely smile. A serious face is identified with power and serious thought. Body language experts also confirm this observation.

But why does it have to be so? Why can't we be normal human beings who like to smile, laugh and share joy? Why this fixation of putting up a serious face to exude position and power.

Let us understand a very simple truth about ourselves. Do we like to be anywhere near a serious or frowning person? Remember once again your childhood days - Did we like the subject taught by a teacher who smiled at us or did we like the subject taught by a teacher who always wore a strict face? Did we like an uncle or aunt who brought cheer whenever they were near or did we like one who wore a frown on their foreheads?

Soft Power in management is all about smooth working styles. Soft Power is about mesmerizing, it is about motivating. And what better way to do it, than with a smile.

Contrary to regular misconception, a smile from the team leader or manager or superior works like a catalyst. A catalyst in increasing faithfulness towards the job, in creating a conducive atmosphere at work, in creating the zeal to give it one's all. Smile, happiness, laughter - these are central to core feelings to humans who work for an Organization and a leader, who stands for the dictum of 'enjoying the job'.

Smile at colleagues and subordinates because your doing so makes them drop their guards. They, so to say, begin to 'warm' up to you. Their mental makeup becomes unguarded. Without fear in their hearts, they begin to trust you. They like being in your presence, they wish to walk the extra mile just to make your plan a success. With a team which is conducive, it becomes much easier for you to be able to concretize your plans and success.

Check out the various polls that take feedbacks regarding 'How happy am I at my job?' Invariably you would find the results tilting towards Organizations which have leaders who wield a Soft Power approach. Money, position, perks do matter, but no one can beat the familiarity and conduciveness of a Smile in Soft Power.

Chapter 23

Constructive Criticism

There come certain times, when unpleasant or rather unpopular activities such as criticism, reprimands, etc become a necessity to ensure that deviated paths are corrected and examples set for the future. However the author strongly advocates elegance and a positive approach even during such trying moments. Soft Power Management does not mean diluting Organizational discipline or policies in any way, it is a methodology of human interaction which ensures a smooth flow of energies and a lightness of approach without compromising on the seriousness of the job at hand.

Have you ever seen an individual who likes to be criticized? I haven't. For sure, no one does. But then sometimes, criticism is important, so that individuals do not stray away from the correct path. So how does one handle such situations?

Let us understand what and why happens in criticism? (A) It tells a person that you are wrong or are treading the wrong path, and (B) it hurts the ego of the individual. Now if this is done in front of colleagues, it hurts the ego all the more. It also then creates feelings of resentment, anger, and hurt among other emotions towards the person criticizing. In this context this means that these feelings would be directed towards you, the team leader or manager. And that is definitely, what no one would like.

This very situation of criticizing or correcting needs to be handled with an approach known as 'Constructive Criticism'. 'Constructive Criticism' is an approach which changes the attitude of the criticized person towards his or her criticizer, while at the same time understanding the fault done. That what we need to focus and work upon. Not all individuals are the types who would change into being appreciative but the resentment, anger and hurt would definitely mellow down and be negated. That will happen when you use Soft Power approaches to address the issue.

Self respect is what is most important for any individual. It means the world, as it stands for years of dignity in the beliefs generated, during one's own existence. And as a mentor, it is most important that you take care of ensuring that you do not hurt this most important feeling. And yet the challenge is to criticize, correct and bring back on track.

The first point to keep in mind is not to criticize in public but talk privately. This one gesture of yours ensures protection of the self respect of the individual as well as him or her looking up to you as someone who means well and is protective in nature. This is the beginning of yielding to your Soft Power. Thereafter, without the intention of blaming for a fault, re-create symbolically the circumstances and steps that went into the individual's mistake. Show him or her, the lacunae or disconnect in the entire episode. Make the individual realize. Thereafter, so as not to spoon feed before hand, ask the individual to show you the alternate approaches he or she could take. This will also help you assess the intellectual and other capabilities of the individual and thereafter guide towards the correct approach. Ensure you keep an overall tab on the individual later without active interference, unless required as a last option. This is constructive criticism wherein you ensure that no one is hurt emotionally and yet gets back into the constructive phase with more enthusiasm and mental vigor.

Chapter 24

Vindictiveness

It is human nature to be upset when something does not go as per our liking. All the more so, if it affects us personally or professionally. A very basic instinct is to lash back, to retaliate, and to pay back in the same coin.

Professionally as a manager, there could rise situations which emotionally hurt and ignite anger in us. It may be triggered by a situation or an individual. The important thing that we need to observe is our own 'reaction' to such a situation. This observing must be from a neutral point of view. Till this neutral view is not obtained, the same may be tinted with the various emotions and hence give us a hampered or distorted view. This neutral view would help us obtain an unbiased understanding of the untoward situation or person. Weighing the various pros and cons with a still mind would help calm the emotions and take the important corrective steps and turn over the situation from being unfavorable to being favorable.

When one becomes vindictive or takes a vindictive stand, he or she has not only let the situation overpower the emotions, they have let the negativity of the situation encompass their whole personality. Their retaliatory action proves beyond doubt that the individual is not in the correct frame of mind. It exposes a weak mental and emotional attitude. A senior person who observes such retaliatory behavior would definitely disapprove of the 'situation-handling' capabilities and a person who is junior would be in fear and awe of such a person. From both people's point of view, the same is unbecoming of the manager.

Instead when a situation or person's action is not according to your liking and which evokes negative strong emotions, just let go and cut off yourself from the situation. Give it a cooling period. Let your own emotions as well as the situation, emotions and actions of others too cool down. Thereafter run the events in your mind in playback mode. Like a movie editor stop the images at appropriate places, observe and analyze those situations. Find the negatives and without getting into the emotional muck and dirtying your consciousness, think of what corrective steps should be used in such situations. Enrich your subconscious with the experience and you would see that you would be able to majorly avoid repetitions of such kind.

Chapter 25

Taskmaster approach

Wrong, inappropriate work which harms the Organization is unpardonable. Corrective measures need to be immediately taken. There can be no arguments on this.

A manager who wields Hard Power takes it up with strong action of demoting or firing and exhibiting to the higher ups as well as subordinates, the zero-tolerance approach. He or she exhibits to the seniors that action has been taken against the erring employee and exhibits to the juniors that in case you make such a mistake, you too would follow in the same path. A lot of people would consider this to be the correct approach. This is most often seen. We will not debate whether this approach is correct or incorrect, but what we will do is exhibit a different approach.

We are all humans. It's not that all actions of ours, over time, have been correct or appropriate. Remember the story of Jesus telling the crowd that only a person, who has never sinned, may pelt the first stone?

For any fault, the first point to consider is 'intention'. Was the fault intentionally done by the subordinate? If it was done so, there are no two ways of handling the situation. Depending on the intensity of the intent, a strong reprimand or even axe is appropriate. Organization and collective goals cannot be handled loosely. It is criminal to do so.

More often however, you would find that the fault was unintentional or out of misunderstanding or misinterpreting the situation. In such a case, you as the senior have two responsibilities - (A) To show the correct path, and (B) To ensure that such a mistake, which pardoned, may never be repeated. As a senior, the first thing is to mentally forgive the person. This is an important step, else your handling of the situation will not be unbiased.

Thereafter analyze the reasons of the mistake - the background of the person, their experience, and exposure and maturity levels. You would need to also consider the reasons from the office or professional front - Was the person wrongly induced to commit this fault by someone else? Was he or she provided wrong information or data which led to faulty analyzing and execution? There could be innumerable such factors each unique to every business or profession. It is important to analyze and understand based on various factors.

Once you have analyzed the reasons of the fault, take the person at fault into confidence. You need to be looked upon by him or her, as a mentor. The person must have full confidence in your just approach and guidance. Thereafter explain and guide the person to the correct approach of handling such a situation. Show the positives of handling the situation in the manner being explained by you. Allow him or her to analyze and rationalize the approach (not just accept it blindly, because you happen to show it). Once the mental analyzing and rationalizing phase is complete, you can be sure that this individual is guided for the rest of the life and would not repeat such a mistake.

With this approach you would have instilled the correct approach into the subconscious mind of the junior, so that it gradually becomes second nature. Not only would such a person be indebted for life, you too would benefit by being correctly guided and protected in future, as per the Principle of Manifesting Thoughts. A good deed always begets a corresponding magnified karma.

Chapter 26

Small things matter

Irrespective of popular beliefs, small things do matter. 'Behavior', in spite of being a very simple and naturally ordinary attribute, holds a very high position in constituting Soft Power.

Your behavior is what you are respected for by others. It is one's behavior in day to day as well as tense scenarios through which the tenacity and internal thought process of an individual gets reflected. This is what either earns respect or earns negativities. Hence it is most important to ensure behavioral corrections, if needed.

Say 'Thank You' to subordinates for each and every small help or contribution they make. The subordinate or colleague may have just helped you with a small input or the chauffer may have opened and held the gate for you or the office peon may have just got a few papers photocopied for you, however small or big a contribution, it must be acknowledged. A small 'thank you' works wonders. It not only is being courteous but it also ensures that in the future the same person would be extremely conducive towards working for you. It is the easiest way of winning over people.

When you talk to your subordinates, use their name in the conversation. To us humans, the sweetest thing which touches our ears is our own name. (Remember when we were small and our favorite uncle used to call us by name to come and grab a cookie or chocolate, that feeling of happiness is what stays, on hearing our own name). Apart from this, it makes the subordinate feel important and wanted. There is a feeling of being one with the conversation, one with the group, of being important to the work. Hence do use this very often.

Note down and remember to congratulate subordinates on their **Birthdays and Anniversaries**. Be it a Birthday, Anniversary or the reaching of a milestone in whichever field, do use the opportunity to congratulate. There are many things that people love to do as a hobby or subjects they deeply care about. Personal milestones in a hobby or on subjects and issues dear to one, matter to each individual. Being acknowledged by a senior makes it all the more important. And, being acknowledged in front of colleagues sweetens the flavor all the more. The feel-good importance takes over for that one day, but it touches much deeper, for longer.

A word of Praise does wonders for a person who has done a good job. Being acknowledged for making a positive contribution is very important for the self-worth of any individual. Say a good word to your mother for the food she doles out, or your wife for the support she offers during your overworked times, or to your husband for taking care of the kids while you have been under office pressure or the person who tends after your garden for the lovely flowers, or anyone for that matter and you would find that they all the more go out of their ways to be helpful and supportive of you.

In the same way it works wonders for a colleague or subordinate when praised or acknowledged for his or her contribution. As mentioned above it works wonders for the self-worth of an individual. And the person acknowledging him or her with such feelings becomes all the more important.

Remember, do not praise just to get something in return. It is important to be genuine in appreciation. Appreciation may be expressed by a simple phone call or an email or just a 'well-done' note. Whatever form you use to express, it must be done genuinely from the heart. You may also praise the person's efforts and contribution when they are not around. That is definitely a strong form of appreciating and acknowledging.

But the best and strongest way of appreciating someone is to take charge, as if it happens to be your natural responsibility, and '*mentor*' him or her. Subtly guiding, honing existing skills, chipping off weaknesses are ways of mentoring and genuinely supporting the person's ride up the corporate ladder and achieving success.

In the following chapter, we shall learn techniques of Breathing, Focusing, Visualization and the 'Meditation on Gold'. This is recommended here so that you are able to effectively apply by *being still and being aware*, the 'Principles of Manifesting Thoughts' in working towards the outcomes you wish to manifest. Lastly the 'Manifesting Thoughts Exercise' will be prescribed which will help in actualization of your thoughts.

Chapter 27

Breathing, Focus, Awareness, Visualization and the Meditation on Gold

Breathing exercise
(This exercise may also be used to calm the mind and emotions in unfavorable circumstances)

Sit in a comfortable position on the chair or on the ground in the lotus pose.

Keep your spine straight.

Breathe in deeply filling your belly (not your chest). Feel the air passing through your nostrils, your throat, your chest region, into your belly. Hold to the count of 3.

Breathe out completely, once again feeling the air emptying out of your belly, moving though your chest, your throat and your nostrils. Hold to the count of 3.

Repeat 10 times.

Relax and allow normal breathing. Just be aware of the surroundings and its elements.

Focus & Awareness exercise
(This exercise helps in one-pointedness)

Be in a relatively calm room.

Take a flower.

In a calm & comfortable pose watch the whole flower.

Do not deviate your eyes or mind from the flower.

Gradually increase the focus and as if magnifying, zoom into a petal.

Feel the texture of the petal through your senses. Feel the softness. Feel the smoothness. Feel the smell. Become one with the flower.

Visualization exercise
(This exercise also helps in developing creativity)

Think of a 'feeling' you want to experience.

It could be the feeling of sitting in a new big car. It could be the feeling of getting the top grades in your exams. It could be the feeling of being on a holiday in a foreign location.

Feel the experience as if it has already happened. Feel the experience in your mind and believe in its reality, its truth. Do not let your mind have any feelings of doubt. Let every pore of your body from the skin on the head to the skin of your feet be immersed in the happiness & contentment of living the experience.

Meditation on Gold

(The oneness of the energy world is felt much better when one practices meditation. Meditation also helps to calm nerves and have a clear thought process. It prepares a discerning mind.)

Sit in a comfortable position, either cross legged on the ground or on a chair. Your spine must be straight. If on a chair, sit further from the back of the chair. No slouching.

Close your eyes and do the Breathing Exercise as mentioned in this chapter before.

Relax the toes of your feet. Relax the lower part & the upper part of your feet. Feel this relaxation moving up towards your ankles, your shin, your calves, your knees. Visualize simultaneously that as each part of your limbs are relaxing, they are brightening up. Let the relaxation build up higher and feel it in your thighs, your groin and your entire hip area relaxing and simultaneously brightening up.

Relax and visualize brightening of your lower abdomen and upper abdomen, your lower, middle and upper back, your chest. Relax your shoulders and your spine. Feel this relaxed feeling now travelling to your upper arms, your elbows your forearms, your wrist, the back of your hand, your palms and into all 10 fingers.

Move your focus back towards your relaxed shoulders and feel the relaxed feeling traveling up towards the back of your head up to the top of your skull. Relax your throat, your tongue, your facial muscles, your eyes, your forehead and this relaxation travels from the front to the top of your skull.

Move your awareness to about 12 inches above your head. With awareness, do the 10 cycles of breathing exercise while keeping your consciousness in this position of 12 inches above your head. Look down upon your body from this vantage point and see that it is shining bright. There are no negative or dark areas anywhere in or around your body. Be still. Be aware. Maintain this stillness for about 2-3 minutes.

Be conscious of the area of 12 inches above your head once again. Imagine as if from your vantage point, liquid golden energy is being poured down into the brain, and it is travelling throughout the brain, towards the back of your head, your forehead, your eyes, tongue, face, your throat, into your shoulders. Simultaneously visualize the area becoming bright golden in color, merging with each and every cell. Let this liquid golden energy travel through your shoulders into your upper arms, your elbows, your forearms, wrists, back of the hand, your palms and into your fingers. Each and every cell is bright golden in color. Focus back on your shoulders and visualize the liquid golden energy travelling down to your chest, your upper and lower abdomen, your upper back, your lower back into your hip region. The area is now bright golden.

Let the liquid golden energy travel down to your groin area into your thighs, your knees, your calves, your shin, into the upper part of the feet and lower part of your feet, into your toes. Feel the liquid gold intermingling and like in the process of osmosis, saturating each and every cell of your body, energizing it with golden energy.

Bring your consciousness back to 12 inches above your head. Look down upon your body and your aura as being thoroughly golden. Be still, Be aware. Maintain this stillness for about 2-3 minutes.

Now we come to the point where we must share the blessings and energies we have received. When we share or give, we ourselves grow further. Hence raise your palms to chest level. Imagine your family in a miniature size in front of you, including yourself and share the golden energies with them. Imagine the golden energies flowing though your palms and enveloping your family in gold. This process of transference of energy is also known as blessing.

Further bless your place of work, all people included. Imagine the golden energies flowing from your hands and enveloping all. Next, bless the area where you stay, your city, your state, your country. You may visualize the Map of your State and Country. Visualize all these in a small size in front of your open palms and being filled with golden energies. Next imagine the Earth, the size of a small ball, between your palms. Visualize it getting brighter and brighter and all humans, animals, land, earth, water and air being energized with this golden energy. Feel the connect through the golden energy with yourself. Feel the oneness.

Let this golden energy further flow into our Universe, the Milky Way where the Planets, their suns and moons are becoming golden. Let the golden energies keep on travelling further into more Universes we are still to find about. Feel the oneness with the golden energies of yourself and the entire universe and beyond. Be still, be aware. Your consciousness is one with the Universal consciousness. Revel in the feeling with joy. Continue being 'one with' the bliss you are experiencing.

After about 5 minutes, be aware of your body and bring your consciousness back to your body. Tap the area of your liver and kidneys with your palms lightly. Get up from your seat and move about. Rub your body so that the golden energies merge with the cells faster. You may walk about a little or do the jumping jacks at one place so that any stiffness eases.

Chapter 28

Manifesting Thoughts Exercise

The Manifesting Thoughts exercise is about visualization. But prior to the visualization and actualization of thoughts, needs to be the imbibing of virtues that lead to proper and responsible manifestations.

In the preceding chapters various values, behavioral changes, emotional and mental states have been touched upon. These values and states need to become part of one's 'thought repertoire'. The stillness and awareness that one achieves, through regular meditation, works as a fertilizer for these values.

The visualization exercise is prescribed here to give you a direction towards manifesting your thoughts. It may be tweaked here and there depending on your individual creativity to maximize the efficacy in your given situation. This is allowed, because every individual is unique and every Conscious mind has a mine of wisdom-tapping power:

- 'Think' about and 'meditate' upon the virtues and behavioral changes you wish to see in yourself and your team.

- Sit in a comfortable position for the 'Meditation on Gold'.

- During the meditation, when you bless you place of work, all people included; visualize the outcomes you wish to see including behavioral changes in yourself and others. Visualize the final outcome as already 'in the present' and *believe* so. See it brighten up with the golden energies you are blessing it with. This golden energy is also fertilizing in nature.

- Once you have completed the above and are in normal day to day working mode, ensure that your belief in the visualized outcome is non-wavering. *Do not over-think* about it and *do not compare* with what you see (esp. if it is a deviation from what you wish for), but '*believe in your belief*' with positive emotions such as thanks, gratitude, happiness and love. This belief must be a constant feeling of yours so that the thought form is part of your Subconscious, which in turn will magnify and manifest the same into your experience. *Believe in your beliefs and do not have an iota of doubt, because doubt is what a pin is to a balloon.*

<u>Epilogue</u>

When we retire from work after giving it our prime of life, what would be the singular most achievement, irrespective of the industry we worked with, that we could look back upon and hold our head high, not with pride but humility; our hearts big not only with happiness but contentment; rest our bones and muscles not of tiredness, but of a job well done?

The answer according to me is giving generations' down-line a mantra for progress and continuity. Of having reared and imbibed the coming generations with values and ethos as building blocks of meaningful lives. Of having guided them, mentored them and sown seeds into their Subconscious of prosperity along with responsible and proper human behavior, based on mutual respect. Only then would they in turn keep the wheel of life spinning and bettering what they have received and further hand it down to their future generations.

Management techniques are needed to run and progress everything in this world - Business Organizations, Researches, Factories and Industries, Economies, Politics, World Forums, et al. On a personal level, we need to even manage our families. The subtle thought changes suggested in this book are a step in the direction of harmoniously managing and can be applied everywhere. On your part, you need to take this progress of harmony forward, resulting in exponential increase of prosperity for all.

This book is my dedication to beautiful lives of our generation and hope it will help them, not only live even more beautiful lives themselves but also prepare an inclusive wholesome world.

May you manifest beautiful lives for yourself and your near-dear ones as well as for generations to come and live a wholesome and prosperous life. May love, peace, joy and fortunes be yours.

Acknowledgements

This book has the blessings and support of so many World Teachers and highly evolved individuals that my heart goes out in thanks, love, respect and gratitude to them. I am indeed blessed. It is with their guidance and revelations that has made possible the release of this book which synthesizes the Principles of Manifesting Thoughts with Management techniques. As Isaac Newton would say "I owe my success to giants, whose shoulders I stand on". Hence my heart goes out in love, thanks, respect and gratitude to the innumerable individuals who have worked in this area of work.

Thanks, love, respect and gratitude to the New Thought Authors and the great Thinkers for showing us the way towards the powers of our Conscious and Subconscious minds and the Law of Attraction. May all of them be blessed for serving humanity.

Thanks, love, respect and gratitude to all in the team of AshMehta & Associates who are making 'Manifesting Thoughts' a flow of energy encompassing and benefitting such a huge number of people through the trainings and the books.

May the blessings keep on flowing through me to humanity and more books in the 'Manifesting Thoughts' series be published soon and be manifested in the Now.

<u>About the Author</u>

Corporate Trainer | Professional Coach | Spiritual Helper

Ashish Mehta, Chief Mentor of AshMehta & Associates, has 23 years experience as an Advertising & Service Industry professional, consultant, entrepreneur, corporate trainer, professional coach and author. He is also a spiritual helper, having practiced Pranic Healing, Arhatic Yoga and various meditations. He is on the Board of Advisors and visiting faculty to the Carolina Institute of

Management & Technology, Kolkata, India.

Ashish brings forth the teachings of Law of Attraction, Thought Management & Visualization by synergizing & empowering most important day to day techniques to win in the corporate world, the social world and the inner worlds - known as the 'Manifesting Thoughts' techniques.

The training modules undertaken by Ashish Mehta are:
- Manifesting Thoughts Effortlessly
- Manifesting successful Study Skills in students
- Manifesting Enviable Personalities & Sowing Leadership seeds
- Manifesting effective Soft Skills
- Manifesting Soft Power Management
- Manifesting Leadership Power
- Manifesting impressive Public Speaking & Presentation skills
- Manifesting effective Body language

The USP of AshMehta trainings is

'Continuance guidance throughout life'. Each and every student of AshMehta trainings can be in touch with him personally, for further personal guidance through email.

'Manifesting Soft Power Management' is the third gift of love from the stable of 'Manifesting Thoughts' techniques. The unique trainings of synergizing Corporate and Life Skills with the Law of Attraction are unheard of before. The resultant success of students who have undertaken the trainings have been phenomenal. This book which you hold in your hands right now is a pioneer in a manner of speaking. The author's first book 'Manifesting Thoughts Effortlessly', which explained the How's and Why's of the Law of Attraction has been widely accepted and acclaimed across the globe. The second book 'Manifesting Impressive Public Speaking & Presentation Skills' has helped a large number of people to overcome their fears and successfully use the techniques prescribed in gaining stature at their official and social meetings and conferences.

The effort of the author is to share his insights and make life worthwhile and live a complete rounded existence.

For more information and for contacting Ashish Mehta, please visit www.ashmehta.in. Please do provide your feedback about the books by pressing 'The Guest Book' button on the website.

You may get in touch with the author as well as find the links to ordering other books released in paperback or e-book formats at the author's website:

Website: http://www.ashmehta.in

Email: ask@ashmehta.in

Facebook:
https://www.facebook.com/ashmehta.in

Twitter:
https://www.twitter.com/Ashmehta_India